SCHIRMER'S LIBRARY
OF MUSICAL CLASSICS

Vol. 1973

GEORG PHILIPP TELEMANN

Concerto in G Major
for Viola and Orchestra

Viola

ISBN 978-0-7935-4872-9

G. SCHIRMER, Inc.

DISTRIBUTED BY

HAL•LEONARD®
CORPORATION
7777 W. BLUEMOUND RD. P.O.BOX 13819 MILWAUKEE, WI 53213

Viola

CONCERTO IN G MAJOR
for Viola and Orchestra

GEORG PHILIPP TELEMANN
(1681-1767)
EDITED BY William Primrose

I

* From m. 48 to the end, Primrose would double the first violin part an octave lower, as notated here.

II

* From m. 70 to the end, Primrose would double the first violin part an octave lower, as notated here.

III

*Primrose made this cut because he thought the chord progression out of the Cadenza enigmatic, the cadence
unnecessary and hindering the flow of the music.

**From m. 27 to the end Primrose would double the first violin part, as notated here.

IV

III

*Primrose made this cut because he thought the chord progression out of the Cadenza enigmatic, and the cadence unnecessary and hindering the flow of the music.

IV

* Primrose played this passage an octave higher.